The Heart of t

The Heart of the Run

Maggie Mackay

Picaroon Poetry
Sheffield, UK

First published in 2018 by Picaroon Poetry

Copyright © Maggie Mackay 2018

All rights reserved. This book or any portion thereof may not be reproduced or used in any manner whatsoever without the express written permission of the publisher except for the use of brief quotations in a book review or scholarly journal.

Maggie Mackay has asserted her right to be identified as the author of this book in accordance with the Copyright, Designs and Patents Act, 1988.

Picaroon Poetry
Sheffield, United Kingdom

ISBN 978-0-244-41176-3

Cover image is via Pixabay and is used under the terms of the CC0 Public Domain License.

To my family from Carsphairn, Paisley and the villa on Gilmore Place

How to Distil a Guid Scotch Malt	9
The Glaistig	10
We are Tightrope Walkers from Tsovkra-1	11
Chilli Pepper	12
Rope Walk	13
The Last Carbonara	14
The Caped Menace	15
Gardener Grafting on the Estate	16
Paisley Pattern	17
this place is everything but dull	18
It's like being thrown in the washing machine again	19
Gouge in the Oak Door	20
Midnight and Saffron	21
Lake Garda	22
Mermaid in Flight	23
Middlemiss Red	24
Malawi Christmas	25
Fitch	26
My Father as a Zephyr	27
Blackout of the Sun Star	28
The Sand Settles and Unsettles my Pulse	29
Winding Wool with Mum	30
Ghazal	31
Acknowledgements	32

How to Distil a Guid Scotch Malt

Separate the Gross from the Subtle
                                    - Hieronymus Brunschwig

Wrap yourself in Mum's dressing gown, its envelope-hug,
pour a dram of *uisge beatha*, sip peppery Talisker peat.

Hear the barley grain grind in the mill, conjure a mash in the steel tun,
a flow into the wash, stroked by hushes and baloo baleerie.

Gloamings on salty coastlines, sweet kiln smoke, skin oil grams,
cloud the floor of the tumbler, climb the sides, pull you into the cask.

Acids blend with ethanol, transform into esters, fruity and aromatic.
A Hebridean sunset copper-pots your tongue, biscuit-beaches rise in your throat.

There's a nip in the air, a lifetime of goodnights fermenting in a kipper fire.
Her arm entwines in yours. She comes home, full flavoured.

Task begun, the heart of the run is now, my middle years of fear and longing.

The Glaistig

We please her at the gloaming by the pond
with a pool of milk in a millstone cradle
not warm at all or scorn-boiled.
Solstice, all seasons, each generation.

We flatten against the standing stone
never knowing how she might appear,
always in her favoured green, plaid wafting in Atlantic surge,
or what her mood might be, grey or blue or gold.

We wait for the wailing or the tricks or her
fixing on our scent. Dragonflies and moths
hover on her heartbeat. Deer dart into the ether,
a distant fiddler strums a jig through the indigo.

We are Tightrope Walkers from Tsovkra-1

Some of our people cat-call if we freeze, panic
high in this mountain place. If they were silent
and not so proud we would look forward,
trust ropes, knots and cables.
If my people didn't stare and tut
we would impress visitors and strangers
who travel far to wonder at our skill.
In this high mountain place
some of my people know neighbours
but no one else, nor roads which lead south.
We are people with the wings of doves,
or eagles or angels. If we are doves we close our eyes
and dance on the line. If we are eagles we balance wings
made with giant fans. If we are angels
we hum praise songs under feather umbrellas.

Chilli Pepper

Hernán Cortés gasps.
        His tongue vibrates in the liquid's pulse;
fluted red, pepper slices burst over his mouth.
        The lobes swell, stuffed with gunpowder fury
  –their flames scream flamenco swirl
the swell of her hips
                on Spanish nights, long ago,
the heave of jasmine and orange...

                He explodes. Heat, heat, so deep.
As she stamps, knuckles hit tables in time,
        the rhythm explodes and peaks;
membranes soaked in garlic oil
                yield fleshy parts fuelled with rapid-fire
staccato cracks of Palomino whip.

A full circle skirt spins, has him reeling.
  Ole! Jaleo!   Then pedicured fingers strum, strum,
        hum, finish him off in the stomach with a punch
    fiercer than the peppers of the Caucasus.

Rope Walk

A place of high industry, a thin long strip of land,
a strip the length of a sailing ship rope.
Hemp-fuelled bottleneck, thick with guttural laughter,
the stramash of creameries and barges,
clang-echo of metal in the forge, the clop of cart horses.
Sparks spiral heavenward. Rough language.

Genesis of dangerous, filthy
demonstrations of tumultuous joy,
the Grassmarket Ball is an annual infamy.
From the roperie of the incendiary Samuel Gilmore,
he sets aflame a fiery-wiry turpentine football
swung, whirled, sling-fashion far into the air.

The Last Carbonara

One ordinary, weekday teatime Sonia,
that friend with the stockpile of life force, rings:
'I've made enough for two. Come over.'

She strains the pasta. 'It's not death,
you see, that worries me,
but how I'll face the pain.'
She cuts the garlic bread, almost too neatly.
'I suppose they'll have something for that.'

The Caped Menace

She's waiting on the Hill Road
for the construction worker
on the short-term contract,
his sweet talk guile.

Her perfect English's only got her so far.
These days it's about foraging for firewood
wielding that axe, being sister-mother to that boy,
when all he wants to do is drum.

Lake Malawi's wink, a planet's orbit away,
holds a promise, salvation or grief,
its shoreline infested
by more men in hyena skins.

Best, dear child,
to have never been so intelligent,
better to have been second born.

Gardener Grafting on the Estate

It's September. The seasonal list birls in his head:
overwinter vegetables, plant alliums,
then fritillaries in the wild wood,
harvest greenhouse fruits,
prune that fig tree, beware of frost.

Home tumbles through him,
a dog rose over the dry stone.
His heart drums with thoughts of the babe,
nursing woe at the old one's passing.
He is a winter gale. He walks on air.

The days shorten into gusts. He clears out
cold frames, nets the pond before leaf-fall.
Summer's seed he pockets to colour the future.
He mends shed roofs before autumn rain,
packs The Edge of Joy in a box of peat.
Gran lives on in the bairn.

Paisley Pattern

My mum whispered at the party, look at little Fern,
restless redhead like her Dad, no lover of shade,

a sunshine soaker, the show-off, the way she tilts her head,
tapping her fingertips over pouty lips. That's my father all over.

A man dies in 1943, gifting prewired traces of movement
to his great granddaughter born on the same day and month,

perhaps antique pulses implanted in protein, poetry in nature
enduring past tuberculosis, factory smoke, malnutrition,

some echo effect or unheralded magic trick,
ripple of a trickle of his gene like an infusion of blood

smouldering, and buoyant out of memory into this room
into her memories, one soul mapped on another, fern fractals.

this place is everything but dull

The summer's flown away with our sister.
Left, us two girls by a silver *dubh lochan*,
you, all pink spike-edged
me, a quiver of moss. We hear silence,
shiver at her earthly ghost call.

You're looking through watery glass
at my plump belly – after seven years,
a niece for you this winter,
along with the rowan berry and frost.
One thread frays. I weave a stronger one.

It's like being thrown in the washing machine again

Acned faces squirm-sneer into the sud glass
as he somersaults through the drum's steel.
White shirts and school ties swirl by,
teenage nasties, as if his mother's returned.

Her leer, a blur through the porthole,
ensnares him once more, traps his three-year-old self
just as before, on the day she was taken away.
His ears burst in that spew and gush, black days,
wash days, flights down corridors of blood.

The swelling skull – which is his – crushes
her marionette pirouette, taunting him
on a childhood spinning top,
its colours running into rainbow smudge.

Gouge in the Oak Door

You seem to think you know enough,
set design and location brief.
But you don't know past shuttered 16th century windows,
crow step gables and cobbled wynds.
Did you hear the pan tile slide,
disintegrate like pink sherbet at my feet,
high storm, last spring?
You seem to think this is a once upon a time.
A lick of paint will pitch us into a blockbuster life?
Slip and slide on December ice,
layered on higgledy-piggledy cobbles.
You weren't there when a car slid full pelt from the Abbey,
down Back Causeway, whacking every parked one like the dodgems.
Modern times, the Post Office closed, a bus once an hour.
You won't discover our community garden,
its fankle of dried leaves, the muddled splash of faded petals,
the cream-white nettle sting crowded by bees?
Have you heard the watering cans gurgle,
the village blether, understated kindnesses?
Have you googled 'plague graves' or 'coffin walk'?
Eavesdropped on Devilla's secrets?
Sat on its lichen-smudged stones, names erased to a fade,
washed by centuries of gales?
You've had no word of Reverend Bishop's slant-angled funeral procession,
nor walked to derelict stacks on Preston Island,
tasted the faint after-trace of furnace smoke,
men's guttural holler, machine-metal clang?
You claim imagination.
Research Carnegie's leaving at the jetty.
He left his heart here.

Midnight and Saffron

So, from the white framed print
her childhood springs.

Ink geometry.
Some artist's pencil cuts between
midnight blue and saffron light.

Two blackhouses stand at right angles,
and, fifty paces east, the Hebridean church
she holds in her heart,
its mouth-music moan, eternal Sunday rest.

Machair shell and sand blow south,
roll in on tides to the shore.
She spots orchids where the corncrake rasps.
Plovers sing on the running water's edge.

On the horizon, she keeps company
with otter, seal and dolphin,
and, through salty wash, gives witness
to her parents' beckoning wave.

Lake Garda

where I fell for Cole's *'Begin the Beguine'*,
where summer soaked me in her heat,
where ribbon-forks of flash-shiver
peppered the heavens, where whizz cracks
burst the stillness of ancient stars.

Dizzy, disappointed with Italian flirts,
I searched the showy sky
where a floating Cima Valdritta snarled.
Below its tip, tail lights flickered,
rubies stolen from Sophia's lakeside villa.
Each pair blinked on roads across the water,
negotiating dangerous turns.

That night I dreamed the scent of mimosa,
the flutter of white sails on glass.
You were cradling me under a lemon tree
and your smile brushed my lips.

Mermaid in Flight

Push against a current
that does not want you.
One last wiggle.
Dive to the depths of Loch Maree,
flick your scaly tail beyond the dark
to a bed as old as the Ice Age.
Inhale salt blown in from the sea.
Be blue, green, turquoise,
riff coral reef pink through your hair.
Chameleon to your core.
Sing soprano songs learned
before you were born
when fisher folk worshipped the idea of you
as they fed on trout and salmon.
Wish human life gone,
him too, you must relinquish,
led to death by your foretelling.
Seek pearls, new friends,
the otter and the diver.
Rest on the Isle at midnight,
make spells in its hermitage.

Middlemiss Red

You are as rare as pink topaz,
so rare that sunlight creeping in at dawn
can halve your life,
as rare as fire that ignites a thousand hearts
or burns the iciest ocean
or bursts the dark sky with shimmer.
You splinter needles of that rarest pink,
warm the crust of this earth
with your imperial hue,
then fade when you've spent
your milliseconds of time,
cast across the universe.

Malawi Christmas

Evening meal shared, sun bled beyond the horizon,
the stone threshold step draws you to the shuttered night.

One poor candle emits yellow light. Christmas stars soak it up,
leaves you sightless and as off-balance as a one-year-old.

Generous hands guide you. The air fills with giggles and hyena cackle.
Under Paul Simon's African skies you squint as the space grows,

falls into your whiteness, close enough to touch,
a blur of radiance, a liberation. You know not what is below your feet.

Above a perigee moon sheds a spotlight, the inky black a backdrop
to silver fury and smoky glow. Flighty besom, stretch out forever

parallel to the heavens, counting stars, drawing constellations,
walking on your back, drunken with possibilities. You long for a star bed.

Fitch

In my midnight I unhook the dust-framed painting,
a childhood spook, a haunting, a fur mask,
and suddenly there's a polecat,
her coat a silkscreen print, soft as her starlit complexion
the dark patches blotted. She is our solitary hunter.
From the gloam of a sand dune, out of oils,
she slouches. Musk charges the room.

This is my mother. She has returned to seek out
her ghost husband, reclaiming him,
he, who was always leafing in libraries.
She drags him by the scruff of his neck,
flicking her tail in the scramble over rockery and log pile.

By dawn she is back in the kitchen,
wielding an iron, as a wife might, pressing office shirts.
I rise to the taste of the polecat's low mewling to her mate.

My Father as a Zephyr

Lightest of all things,
he blows in light of a perpetual spring,
scatters the salty Clyde with early summer breezes,
with seaweed fronds on soft foam,
fruit of our childhood holidays.
His soft stirring smile greets aquamarine.
His wind-song dances on fiddle strings, sotto.
The west wind restores dear ones
with a tease, a coorie-in, a purr.

Blackout of the Sun Star

crumbling mortar on windowsill
                heartsore at your absence
        meteor rushing towards Earth
you at my centre, I orbit to the end of time
             raindrops gather below clouds
quarrels like ferrets in a sack
      neighbour's children gathering pebbles
for days, the sky expanding to dusty grey
      regret a stone in my pocket
                   sighs for want of peace
time stretches as far as Saturn's rings

The Sand Settles and Unsettles my Pulse

The desert sand nestles in the cracks between my toes,
        rests in the grooves of my nails. It blasts
the intricate geometry of the Persian rug you gifted me,
        smudges, tramples me through the pores
of skirting boards which sandbag ground in the face of flood.
        My dream castle lists beneath my feet.

Sand sifts into my books, blue, red, flecked with gold fire.
        As their spines line up like sentries, I am a dustcover
wrapped by dunes pressing my shoulders to my toes.
        Dream castles float in the damp tide-lap.
This intruder waits, deep store-darkened in the camphor chest,
        column-stacked against my bedroom wall,
graining the white picture frame.

Imp-sand flows under the door like a river in spate,
        splashes mesmerising patterns of an underground spring
fathoms deep in the earth's crust that merge on window and sill,
        washing your persistent voice from the stale air,
out of waves which wiped dream castles to nothing.

My heart is a sandpit.

Winding Wool with Mum

The touch of any wool, its subtle down,
gold inner warmth, slips through my pores.
Like sunshine through these blinds, it rolls out
from a mass of folds. Then, dyed
with reds and blues and greens and time,
in threads and cloth, it is felt.

Folded here, your cashmere wrap recalls the hours
we spent in peace winding long skeins around
the kitchen chair's waist. With nods and smiles
your fingers and mine wove patterns, tied knots,
spinning our unspoken strands of love.

Your hands can only slip a squeeze these days
or clutch the chair to rise and clasp the mohair rug.
When you call me darling, I wind straight back to home.

Ghazal

I've not been schooled in how to wait, precious mother,
to grasp your three simple words *I'll be waiting*, precious mother.

The grey-green of your eyes holds me fast.
The flutter of your wing gives me strength, precious mother.

My prayers return you as a swallow to the telephone wire's tightrope
but you grow restless with the harvest moon, precious mother.

My wee heart is a fledgling boom under the fluff of feather.
I hear you tut-cheep at my impatience, precious mother.

I might be a jilted lover, a bridal footsteps' echo on ancient stone
waiting for the rainbow's road end, precious mother.

In my dreams you wait for me to open like a perfumed June rose,
budding in early morning dew, precious mother.

You plant seeds of longing on my path, cornflower and love-in-a-mist,
as we dance to a celebration jig, precious mother.

Your smile urges me forward, no more waiting this time
as you call from the edge of my bed, *fly to me, Margaret.*

Acknowledgements

Some of the poems, or versions of them were published in Twelve Days of Christmas 2017 on *Ink, Sweat &Tears, Amaryllis, Yorkmix, Reach Poetry, Prole, Rat's Ass Review, Three Drops from a Cauldron, Unpsychology, Visual Verse,* and *The Writers' Café Magazine.*

'Midnight and Saffron' was commended by Alison Lock in the Mothers' Milk Writing Prize, 2017.

Huge thanks are due to Maureen Cullen, Sonia Cameron at the OU, Jean Sprackland at MMU and the group of 52, 2014. Helen Ivory and Marie Lightman are special people too.

Warmest thanks to Kate Garrett for her faith in my writing.